Majority Interim Report: Benghazi Investigation Update

Chairman Howard P. "Buck" McKeon

Committee on Armed Services

February 2014

Executive Summary

Immediately after the terrorist attack in Benghazi, Libya on September 11, 2012, the Committee on Armed Services began an ongoing extensive effort to evaluate the response of the Department of Defense (DOD). In addition to assessing how the Department reacted, the committee seeks to determine what preparations the U.S. military had made for the possibility of an attack in Libya, and what arrangements have subsequently been put into place to minimize the possibility of a similar recurrence.

To undertake the committee's review, Chairman Howard P. "Buck" McKeon has directed the Oversight and Investigations subcommittee to work alongside the full committee. As a result, this report expresses the views of Chairman McKeon, Vice Chairman Mac Thornberry, Rep. Martha Roby (who was the chairman of the Oversight and Investigations subcommittee until December 2013), and the five majority members of that subcommittee. These eight members are collectively referred to as the "majority members" in this report.

This report should be considered one component of continuing comprehensive Benghazi-related oversight underway in the U.S. House of Representatives. In keeping with the committee's jurisdiction, however, this document addresses only the activities and actions of personnel in DOD. To date, committee staff has reviewed thousands of pages of written material (including classified emails and situation reports) made available by DOD. Staff has also held three classified staff briefings, and two classified interviews. Members have participated in two open hearings, and seven additional classified briefings. In undertaking this work, the committee has met with and received information from military personnel in the entire chain of command in connection with Benghazi: from those on the ground at the time of the attack to the nation's senior-most uniformed leader.

While the committee's inquiry continues, the majority members believe that information gathered to date reaffirm the relevant findings in the *Interim Progress Report for the Members of the Republican Conference on the Events Surrounding the September 11, 2012 Terrorist Attack in Benghazi, Libya* issued in April 2013 by the five committees with jurisdiction in the U.S. House of Representatives. Further, based on its activities undertaken since the release of that report, majority members make the six findings listed on the following page.

Findings

I. In assessing military posture in anticipation of the September 11 anniversary, White House officials failed to comprehend or ignored the dramatically deteriorating security situation in Libya and the growing threat to U.S. interests in the region. Official public statements seem to have exaggerated the extent and rigor of the security assessment conducted at the time.

II. U.S. personnel in Benghazi were woefully vulnerable in September 2012 because a.) the administration did not direct a change in military force posture, b.) there was no intelligence of a specific "imminent" threat in Libya, and c.) the Department of State, which has primary responsibility for diplomatic security, favored a reduction of Department of Defense security personnel in Libya before the attack.

III. Defense Department officials believed nearly from the outset of violence in Benghazi that it was a terrorist attack rather than a protest gone awry, and the President subsequently permitted the military to respond with minimal direction.

IV. The U.S. military's response to the Benghazi attack was severely degraded because of the location and readiness posture of U.S. forces, and because of lack of clarity about how the terrorist action was unfolding. However, given the uncertainty about the prospective length and scope of the attack, military commanders did not take all possible steps to prepare for a more extended operation.

V. There was no "stand down" order issued to U.S. military personnel in Tripoli who sought to join the fight in Benghazi. However, because official reviews after the attack were not sufficiently comprehensive, there was confusion about the roles and responsibilities of these individuals.

VI. The Department of Defense is working to correct many weaknesses revealed by the Benghazi attack, but the global security situation is still deteriorating and military resources continue to decline.

Background

Immediately after the terrorist attack in Benghazi, Libya on September 11, 2012, the Committee on Armed Services began an ongoing extensive effort to evaluate the response of the Department of Defense (DOD). In addition to assessing how the Department reacted to the terrorist strike that killed Ambassador J. Christopher Stevens, State Department employee Sean Smith, and CIA security personnel Tyrone Woods, and Glen Doherty, the committee seeks to determine what preparations the U.S. military had made for the possibility of an attack in Libya, and what arrangements have subsequently been put into place to minimize the possibility of a similar recurrence.

In connection with the Benghazi-related matters within its purview, Chairman Howard P. "Buck" McKeon has made it clear to DOD that the committee intends to address the topic "thoroughly, authoritatively, and conclusively."[1] To undertake the committee's review, Chairman McKeon has directed the Oversight and Investigations subcommittee to work alongside the full committee. This approach facilitates the evaluation of many important broad subjects by the larger body, while applying the subcommittee's specialized resources to an in-depth review of specific questions. As a result, this report expresses the views of Chairman McKeon, Vice Chairman Mac Thornberry, Rep. Martha Roby (who was the chairman of the Oversight and Investigations subcommittee until December 2013), and the five majority members of that subcommittee. Hereafter, these eight Members of Congress are referred to as "the majority members."

This report should be considered one component of continuing comprehensive Benghazi-related oversight underway in the U.S. House of Representatives. In keeping with the committee's jurisdiction, this document addresses only the activities and actions of personnel in DOD.[2] However, consistent with the rules of the House of Representatives, committees with authority over the White House, Department of State, the intelligence community, the Federal

---

[1] See Howard P. "Buck" McKeon, Chairman, Committee on Armed Services letter to Chuck Hagel, Secretary of Defense, May 14, 2013.

[2] An "Accountability Review Board" (ARB) empanelled by then-Secretary of State Hillary Clinton primarily examined State Department actions, procedures and personnel in Benghazi. Nonetheless, the Board concluded "there simply was not enough time given the speed of the attacks for armed U.S. military assets to have made a difference." (See U.S. Department of State, unclassified Accountability Review Board report, December 2012, pp. 1, 10 [hereafter "ARB Report"].) In a statement to the Senate Armed Services Committee in February 2013, then-Secretary of Defense Leon Panetta similarly declared, "I firmly believe that the Department of Defense and the U.S. Armed Forces did all we could do in the response to the attacks in Benghazi. We employed every asset at our disposal that could have been used to help save lives of our American colleagues." Secretary Panetta also said "[a]lthough we had forces deployed to the region, time, distance, the lack of an adequate warning, [and] events that moved very quickly on the ground prevented a more immediate response. . . . Before, during, and after the attack, every request the Department of Defense received we . . . accomplished." (See Hearing Transcript, U.S. Senate, Committee on Armed Services, "Hearing to Receive Testimony on Department of Defense's Response to the Attack on U.S. Facilities in Benghazi, Libya, and the Findings of its Internal Review Following the Attack," February 7, 2013, p. 7 (hereafter "Senate Hearing"). For General Martin Dempsey's impressions of the extent of the ARB's evaluation of military matters, see Briefing Transcript (redacted), U.S. House of Representatives, Committee on Armed Services, Subcommittee on Oversight and Investigations, "The Defense Department's Force Posture in Anticipation of September 12, 2012," October 10, 2013, p. 31 (hereafter "Dempsey Briefing").

Bureau of Investigation, and other federal agencies are conducting parallel and closely coordinated reviews.[3]

Material reviewed

To date, committee staff has reviewed thousands of pages of written material (including classified emails and situation reports) made available by DOD. Staff has also held three classified staff briefings, and two classified interviews. Members have participated in two open hearings, and seven additional classified briefings.

General Martin Dempsey (the chairman of the Joint Chiefs of Staff), General Carter Ham (who commanded U.S. Africa Command [AFRICOM] at the time of the attack), other general and flag officers, and senior civilian defense officials appeared before the committee. They provided information about DOD actions in connection with the attack, and described constraints on deploying other forces, including drones and fighter aircraft. The committee also heard from field-grade officers who were in Libya at the time, or in contact with those who were, to discern their understanding of events and the Department's operational limitations. Thus, the committee has met with and received information from military personnel in the entire chain of command in connection with Benghazi: from those on the ground at the time of the attack to the nation's senior-most uniformed leader.

In conjunction with the Committee on Oversight and Government Reform, the Armed Services Committee is arranging for staff to interview additional witnesses in coming weeks, including individuals who were involved in responding to the Benghazi events and other officials. Some individuals who have already provided information will appear for further questioning and clarification.

Classification issues

The assessment of military operations, planning, and contingency actions necessarily involves classified information. Therefore, the committee has convened some events in a classified setting. This arrangement, coupled with the evaluation of classified documents, allows the committee and its staff to gain a comprehensive understanding of the matters at hand.

The findings set forth in this report rest on the totality of information (classified or not) available to the committee as of this time. At the committee's request, the Department of Defense has identified the classified portions of approximately 450 pages of official transcripts of committee briefings. Doing so allows the committee to cite the balance of this material in its public statements. The transcripts, with classified information redacted, have been released in conjunction with this report.

---

[3] In connection with the committee's Benghazi-related activities, the chairmen and ranking members of other relevant Congressional committees, along with certain select cleared staff have been invited to attend committee events. In addition, arrangements have been made to accommodate other members of the House of Representatives. All those who attended have been given the opportunity to participate fully; to pose questions, and evaluate information provided. The committee also makes transcripts and other documents available to members who seek clarification or additional exposure to the material collected.

The majority members make three important notes about how the classified information was handled by DOD. First, the committee retains possession of the original transcripts and knows what specific information was marked as classified. Second, the majority members have no reason to believe the Department's decisions were guided by anything other than a good-faith effort to apply relevant law and classification guidance; there is no indication that any material is being improperly kept from the public. Third, the majority members assess that none of the redacted items contravene or weaken the findings set forth below. If redacted material has any relevance to a report finding, it strengthens rather than undercuts the assessment set forth.[4]

Other relevant information

In addition to material provided directly to the committee by DOD, to produce this report the committee has also considered information gathered by other Congressional committees or appearing in the public domain.[5] It is also necessary to note that this report emphasizes significant aspects of the information evaluated by the committee to date. It is not, however, meant to be an exhaustive catalog or evaluation of every point or detail contained in this material.

---

[4] The committee objected to one redaction in a transcript reviewed by DOD. The Department readily conceded this material was withheld by mistake and conveyed a corrected transcript to the committee. Separately, the committee is aware of miscellaneous mistakes, including minor transcription errors caused by audio quality or the transcriptionist's unfamiliarity with certain names, terms, and/or abbreviations. Because they do not substantively change the information conveyed, no effort has been made to correct these items in the transcripts. Footnotes in this document indicate when alterations have been made for spelling or punctuation.

[5] This includes U.S. Senate, Select Committee on Intelligence, "Review of the Terrorist Attacks on U.S. Facilities in Benghazi, Libya, September 11-12, 2012, Together with Additional Views," January 15, 2014 (Hereafter "Review of the Terrorist Attacks"); David D. Kirkpatrick, "A Deadly Mix in Benghazi," *New York Times*, December 28, 2013; Fred Burton and Samuel M. Katz, *Under Fire: the Untold Story of the Attack in Benghazi* (New York: St. Martin's Press, 2013) and the since-discredited book by "Morgan Jones" and Damien Lewis, *The Embassy House: the Explosive Eyewitness Account of the Libyan Embassy Siege by the Soldier Who Was There* (New York: Threshold Editions, 2013).

Findings

While the committee's inquiry continues, the majority members believe that information gathered to date reaffirm the relevant findings in the *Interim Progress Report for the Members of the Republican Conference on the Events Surrounding the September 11, 2012 Terrorist Attack in Benghazi, Libya* issued in April 2013 by the five committees with jurisdiction in the U.S. House of Representatives.[6] Further, based on its activities undertaken since the release of that report, majority members make the following findings:

I. In assessing military posture in anticipation of the September 11 anniversary, White House officials failed to comprehend or ignored the dramatically deteriorating security situation in Libya and the growing threat to U.S. interests in the region. Official public statements seem to have exaggerated the extent and rigor of the security assessment conducted at the time.

After Muammar Gaddafi was toppled in October 2011, Libya's continued troubles were well known to the public and policy makers. The interim government that had come to power struggled to exercise central control over Libya. The country's borders were insecure, weapons were plentiful, and infighting raged. In eastern Libya especially, as the Department of State later described, there was "lawlessness" and "political violence," including "assassinations targeting former regime officials."[7]

This tumult was obvious in the city of Benghazi. In the eighteen months before September 2012, there were nearly twenty violent incidents targeting U.S. or western interests there. British and UN diplomats were attacked (eventually sparking the United Kingdom to close its mission in June 2012), and the walls surrounding U.S. diplomatic complex (known as the Special Mission Compound) were hit by two explosive devices. A group that claimed responsibility for a rocket attack on a Red Cross building subsequently issued a threat against the United States.[8] Militant training camps had also been established in Libya, and Al Qaeda's influence seemed to be growing.[9]

If this public information was insufficient to cause grave concern to policy makers, those privy to classified intelligence evaluations should have been even more alarmed. For example, a July 2012 Central Intelligence Agency assessment (evocatively entitled "Libya: Al-Qa'ida Establishing Sanctuary") ominously declared "Al-Qa'ida-affiliated groups and associates are exploiting the permissive security environment in Libya to enhance their capabilities and expand

---

[6] "Interim Progress Report for the Members of the House Republican Conference on the Events Surrounding the September 11, 20-12 Terrorist Attacks in Benghazi, Libya," April 23, 2013, (hereafter "Interim Progress Report").
[7] ARB Report, p. 15.
[8] ARB Report, pp. 15-16.
[9] One unclassified U.S. government report issued in August 2012 identified a former Guantanamo detainee as one of the possible "principal leaders" of the clandestine network the terrorist group was "likely" be developing in Libya. (See "Al-Qaeda in Libya: A Profile," Library of Congress, August 2012, especially pp. 2-17.) For a discussion of the process to reduce population of the Guantanamo detention facility and the fact that some former detainees are believed to have reengaged in terrorist activities, see Committee on Armed Services, Subcommittee on Oversight and Investigations, *Leaving Guantanamo: Policies, Pressures, and Detainees Returning to the Fight*, (Washington DC: U.S. Government Printing Office, 2012).

their operational reach."[10] Indeed, as a bipartisan report of the Select Committee on Intelligence in the U.S. Senate has noted, in the months before the Benghazi attack, the U.S. Intelligence Community circulated "hundreds" of reports (including one issued just four days before the attack) "warning that militias and terrorist and affiliated groups had the capability and intent to strike U.S. and Western facilities and personnel in Libya."[11]

Amidst all this, on September 10, 2012, the Office of the Press Secretary at the White House released a statement summarizing a meeting the President convened earlier that day. The White House described it as an opportunity for the President to confer "with senior Administration officials on our preparedness and security posture" in advance of the anniversary of the 2001 terrorist attacks on the United States.[12] The press secretary's office reported that:

> Over the past month, Assistant to the President for Homeland Security and Counterterrorism John Brennan has convened numerous meetings to review security measures in place.[13]

In light of these evaluations, the press office declared:

> The President heard from key national security principals on our preparedness and security posture on the eve of the eleventh anniversary of September 11th. . . . [T]he President and the Principals discussed specific measures we are taking in the Homeland to prevent 9/11 related attacks as well as the steps taken to protect U.S. persons and facilities abroad, as well as force protection. The President reiterated that Departments and agencies must do everything possible to protect the American people, both at home and abroad.[14]

This is a commendable sentiment and describes actions expected of the commander-in-chief. However, majority member believe that this description may have overstated the extent of the White House involvement and the rigor of its posture analysis.

In his briefing to the committee, General Dempsey recalled that discussions about the nation's security posture took place in "a conference call" with the President.[15] He recounted that the call first recapped specific "threats to the homeland," reviewed the situation in "Tunisia, Egypt and Sudan" (but not Libya), and then "addressed, in general, our force posture both in the Gulf and in North Africa."[16] However, General Dempsey and Leon Panetta, then the Secretary of Defense, also testified to the Senate Armed Services Committee (SASC) in February 2013 that they attended a White House meeting on September 10, 2012. Secretary Panetta described it

---

[10] Review of the Terrorist Attacks, p. 10.

[11] Review of the Terrorist Attacks, p. 9. Committee staff has reviewed reporting from the Defense Intelligence Agency in this period.

[12] Office of the Press Secretary, The White House, "Readout of the President's Meeting with Senior Administration Officials on Our Preparedness and Security Posture on the Eleventh Anniversary of September 11th," September 10, 2012 (hereafter "White House Readout"). Note: the capitalization has been changed from the original source.

[13] White House Readout.

[14] White House Readout.

[15] Dempsey Briefing, p. 20.

[16] Dempsey Briefing, pp. 21-22.

as a gathering that "looked at what the potential threats were as a result of going into September 11," while General Dempsey said it was a "routine monthly review of counterterror operations worldwide."[17]

Regardless of the specifics, General Dempsey told the committee he had been "aware of" the White House's posture evaluation touted in the press release, but did not remember "personally" taking part in it. He said the vice chairman or another senior officer from the Joint Staff was involved in his stead.[18] As for AFRICOM, when General Ham was asked in a committee briefing "did anyone in DOD, the White House, or national security staff, including Mr. Brennan, review the force posture with you," he answered "I do not recall any" such conversations.[19]

It is difficult to reconcile these various descriptions. However, the committee seeks further details on these one or two telephone or in-person consultations and information on the discrete military preparations (if any) that were sparked as a result. But, it is important to note that, when the committee asked if certain specialized military units had been ordered to shorten their potential response times as a consequence of the pre-September 11 discussions, General Dempsey reported that neither Secretary Panetta nor he had directed this.[20] Nonetheless, General Ham told the committee he had "a discussion" with General Dempsey about the defense posture being assumed in AFRICOM in advance of September 11, 2012.[21]

Secretary Panetta's role

Secretary Panetta and his senior-most assistants seem to have been especially prepared to evaluate defensive preparations in and around North Africa at the time. Secretary Panetta and General Ham visited Libya in December 2011. In describing the trip to the committee, General Ham noted the two met with embassy personnel, including the defense attaché, and other officials. The general said that after the visit, he and the secretary also had "many subsequent discussions" about what they observed.[22] Although General Ham cautioned that he was not speaking for Secretary Panetta, he recounted to the committee that it was his impression that the secretary shared the general's sense that a weakening Libyan government was a "dangerous development" which "created opportunities for Al Qaeda and other Islamic extremist organizations to, in some cases, reinsert themselves or operatives into Libya."[23] General Ham said he shared these views with General Dempsey as well.[24]

For his part, General Dempsey recalled that upon the secretary's return, the secretary "briefed all of us, to include his staff, on his visit to Libya." General Dempsey said the secretary

---

[17] Senate Hearing, p. 16.
[18] Dempsey Briefing, p. 21.
[19] Briefing Transcript (redacted), U.S. House of Representatives, Committee on Armed Services, Subcommittee on Oversight and Investigations, "AFRICOM and SOCAFRICA and the Terrorist Attacks in Benghazi, Libya on September 11, 2012," June 26, 2013, p. 69 (hereafter "AFRICOM and SOCAFRICA Briefing").
[20] Dempsey Briefing, p. 47.
[21] AFRICOM and SOCAFRICA Briefing, p. 28.
[22] AFRICOM and SOCAFRICA Briefing, p. 16 (quote), p. 56.
[23] AFRICOM and SOCAFRICA Briefing, p. 16. Punctuation added for clarity.
[24] AFRICOM and SOCAFRICA Briefing, p. 17.

spoke "about how to build security forces in Libya" and said there was no discussion "specifically" about the embassy or the Special Mission Compound (SMC), the U.S. diplomatic facility in Benghazi.[25]

Libya handled differently than Yemen

It seems the prevailing assessment within the Department of Defense after December 2011 was that the security situation in Libya was poor and growing worse. According to General Dempsey's testimony to the Senate, General Ham had advised him of his impressions of deteriorating events.[26] Because this assessment was apparently widely shared by and discussed among senior uniformed and civilian leaders, and because it was largely based upon their personal observations, it seems likely this view was conveyed to the White House. Yet, administration decision makers were apparently reluctant to discuss publicly the deteriorating security situation in Libya or make changes in the U.S. diplomatic presence or military force posture that might have mitigated the dangers there. The inaction in Libya is in stark contrast to security improvements instituted elsewhere.

For example, before September 11, 2012, additional U.S. military forces were dispatched to Yemen at the urging of the Department of State.[27] Yet at the time, Yemen, although an extraordinarily difficult location beset with many dangers, could have been considered to be *relatively more* secure than Libya. The decision to act in Yemen but not in Libya is even more puzzling in light of the history and pattern of attacks against U.S. and western targets in Libya, the fact the U.S. embassy in Tripoli did not have a U.S. Marine security guard detachment, and Secretary Panetta's personal knowledge of the dire circumstances there.

It may be that the reluctance to act more forcefully in Libya is related to the administration's general aversion to deploying ground troops.[28] Further inquiry may yield additional details about Secretary Panetta's understanding of the Libyan situation, counsel he may have provided to the White House or others in the executive branch, and his assessment of Mr. Brennan's posture review before the attack. The committee has contacted the secretary to receive his comments on these matters. Similarly, Mr. Brennan, and other past or present

---

[25] Dempsey Briefing, p. 8. Punctuation added for clarity. In some publications, the SMC is alternatively referred to as a "Temporary Mission Facility" or TMF.

[26] Senate Hearing, pp. 21 26-27, 29, 37, 49-50.

[27] Senate Hearing, pp. 26, 72-73.

[28] Three Brookings Institution scholars, including two who served the president, have written that he "clearly brought to office a wariness about American interventionism." (See Martin S. Indyk, Kenneth G. Lieberthal, and Michael E. O'Hanlon, *Bending History: Barack Obama's Foreign Policy* (Washington: Brookings Institution Press, 2012), p. 70.) Similarly, analyst Peter Beinart observes that the Obama administration, in many instances instead of deploying ground troops, is "trying to secure our interest from the sea, the air, and by equipping our allies." (Quoted in Lloyd D. Gardner, *Killing Machine: The American Presidency in the Age of Drone Warfare* (New York: New Press, 2013), p. 194.) Political scientist Henry Nau also assesses that the administration typically "deploys forces from offshore, thereby minimizing boots on the ground." (See Henry R. Nau, "The Jigsaw Puzzle & the Chessboard," *Commentary*, May 2012). Nau concludes elsewhere that "[t]he use of force only when it is absolutely necessary does not minimize risks, it leads to much bigger risks later on." (See Henry R. Nau, "Obama's Foreign Policy," *Policy Review*, April-May 2010.) One exception to a reluctance to embrace troop deployments is reported in Craig Whitlock, "U.S. advisers are first to be sent to Somalia since 1993," *Washington Post*, January 11, 2014.

National Security Council and White House staffers can be a source of information for those committees inquiring into the role of the White House and NSC in reviewing the security posture and the decision not to dispatch more military forces to Libya before September 11, 2012.

II. U.S. personnel in Benghazi were woefully vulnerable in September 2012 because a.) the administration did not direct a change in military force posture, b.) there was no intelligence of a specific "imminent" threat in Libya, and c.) the Department of State, which has primary responsibility for diplomatic security, favored a reduction of Department of Defense security personnel in Libya before the attack.

Administration did not mandate a change in force posture

In a written statement provided to SASC in February 2013, General Dempsey described the U.S. military's worldwide force posture at the time of the Benghazi attack. He said:

> we were postured to respond to a wide array of general threats around the globe. We positioned our forces in a way that was informed by and consistent with available threat estimates.[29]

Similarly, General Ham explained to the House Armed Services Committee that his challenge in AFRICOM was to determine how to "best posture forces that could be able to respond" to an emergency across "a vast [geographical] area" in which there was "a lot of uncertainty and . . . a couple of pockets of really heightened concern."[30]

As noted, above, the majority members believe the White House's pre-September 11 security review failed in that it did not result in direction to the Department of Defense to react to the deteriorating security environment in Libya. Major General (USAF) Darryl Roberson, Vice Director, Operations (J-3), Joint Staff, briefed the committee that "based on the indications and warnings at the time," DOD's force laydown in the region (and elsewhere around the world) changed little in preparation for September 11, 2012. Mr. Garry Reid, the Principal Deputy Assistant Secretary of Defense for Special Operations and Low-Intensity Conflict, similarly told the committee that DOD was "postured for a wide range of contingencies" on September 11, 2012. In part, this was because after 2001, there had never been another terrorist attack on a September 11, and thus there was little evidence that this date should pose an extraordinary concern.[31]

---

[29] "Statement of General Martin E. Dempsey, USA, Chairman , Joint Chiefs of Staff, Before the Senate Armed Services Committee, Benghazi," February 7, 2013, p. 4 (hereafter "Dempsey Statement"). In a colloquy with the Senate Armed Services Committee, General Dempsey further explained the posture was based on information from the intelligence community and State Department, including their senior-most representatives in the country. See Senate Hearing, p. 21.

[30] AFRICOM and SOCAFRICA Briefing, p. 64. General Ham also invoked the absence of warning of imminent attack. See Carter Ham, "AFRICOM: The Next Afghanistan," Aspen Institute (Aspen, Colorado), July 19, 2013 (video available at http://www.youtube.com/watch?v=sIIJ-JbeLRg) (hereafter "Aspen Remarks").

[31] Briefing Transcript (redacted), U.S. House of Representatives, Committee on Armed Services, Subcommittee on Oversight and Investigations, "Benghazi Briefing," May 21, 2013, Part I, pp. 15, 33 (hereafter "May Benghazi Briefing, Part I"). See also comments by Rear Admiral Brian Losey in AFRICOM and SOCAFRICA Briefing, pp. 115-116. General Ham, however, suggested there was acute sensitivity to potential threats keyed to the September 11 anniversary in public remarks he made in July 2013. See Aspen Remarks.

Absence of an imminent threat

Mr. Reid said "although there were threat warnings across the board, there were no specific indications of an imminent attack" in Benghazi.[32] The director of the Defense Intelligence Agency (DIA) echoed this. In correspondence to the committee, Lieutenant General Michael Flynn reported that

> prior to September 11, 2012, DIA neither formally nor informally advised the Department of State or any other agency about any specific threat to the United States personnel in Libya.[33]

Indeed, General Dempsey noted that "[l]eading up to and throughout the day of the attack . . . I had received reports of possible threats to U.S. interests including in Sana'a, Khartoum, Islamabad, Peshawar, Kabul, Cairo, and Baghdad," but he also emphasized that he "didn't receive any specific reports of imminent threats to U.S. personnel or facilities in Benghazi."[34] General Dempsey told the committee the lack of a specific warning was critical in making threat assessments.[35]

The majority members note the absence of an *imminent* threat in Benghazi. But, it is commonsensical to assume that if the United States received greater warning about a specific impending attack, its forces would have been better prepared. In Benghazi, U.S. forces were confronted with the unexpected, and the committee is necessarily focused on how the nation's military responded to this *unanticipated* scenario.

Majority members also note that General Dempsey explained to the Senate that "U.S. facilities in many countries throughout the Africa Command and Central Command areas were operating under heightened force protection levels" on September 11, 2012.[36] Thus, although the administration did not mandate any broader defense changes, the Department of Defense, apparently on its own initiative, instituted procedures meant to safeguard personnel at their duty stations outside the United States.

Department of State's primary responsibility for diplomatic security decisions

Regardless of DOD's preparations before September 11, it is essential to acknowledge that the Department of State has primary responsibility for embassy security. This includes identifying to DOD those diplomatic posts that require additional measures or a prospective

---

[32] May Benghazi Briefing, Part I, p. 57. See also remarks by General Carter Ham and Rear Admiral Brian Losey in AFRICOM and SOCAFRICA Briefing, pp. 11, 19, 114.

[33] Lieutenant General Michael T. Flynn, Director, Defense Intelligence Agency, letter to Howard P. "Buck" McKeon, Chairman, Committee on Armed Services, October 31, 2012. He specified this did not include "formal DIA analytical products." See Ibid.

[34] Dempsey Briefing, p. 6.

[35] Dempsey Briefing, pp. 27-28

[36] Dempsey Statement.

emergency response.[37] DIA provides information to the Department of State to assist in these determinations. Lieutenant General Flynn specified to the committee four occasions in which DIA analysts discussed "the security situation in Libya with representatives of the Department of State." He said this included providing briefings to Ambassador J. Christopher Stevens in May 2012 on "Libyan security sector development, [and] terrorist threats from Libya."[38]

Security Support Team reduction

State Department officials in Libya apparently understood the dangers. As noted in the Interim Progress Report, on several occasions in 2012 Ambassador Stevens and others at the U.S. embassy stressed within the Department of State the inadequacy of security in Libya and outlined the need for additional personnel.[39] In fact, however, in the weeks before the attack there was a decrease in the modest U.S. military presence there. For many months, there was a sixteen-person Special Forces unit, known as the Security Support Team or the Site Security Team (SST), at the embassy in Tripoli. This unit was involved with protecting the U.S. compound. In August 2012, however, DOD briefed that at the request of the Department of State, this unit was reduced to four personnel and their focus changed to training Libyan forces.[40] General Ham told the committee that this reduction and transition was done despite his offer to retain the larger number.[41]

---

[37] Briefing Transcript (redacted), U.S. House of Representatives, Committee on Armed Services, Subcommittee on Oversight and Investigations, "Benghazi Briefing," May 21, 2013, Part II, p. 46 (hereafter "May Benghazi Briefing, Part II"); May Benghazi Briefing, Part I, pp. 42-44, 65-71; Senate Hearing, pp. 8, 55.

[38] Lieutenant General Flynn letter to Chairman McKeon.

[39] Interim Progress Report, pp. 7-10.

[40] AFRICOM and SOCAFRICA Briefing, pp. 54, 78-79, 93-95, 125, and 138-140; Hearing Transcript, U.S. House of Representatives, Committee on Oversight and Government Reform, "Benghazi: Exposing Failure and Recognizing Courage," May 8, 2013, *CQ Congressional Transcripts,* pp. 32-33 (hereafter "Oversight Hearing"); Hearing Transcript, U.S. Senate, Budget Committee, "Hearing on President Obama's Fiscal 2014 Budget Proposal for the Department of Defense," June 12, 2013, *CQ Congressional Transcripts*, p. 29 (hereafter "Senate Budget Hearing"); and untitled written statement Lieutenant Colonel (USA) Andrew Wood, U.S. House of Representatives, Committee on Oversight and Government Reform, October 10, 2012 (Lieutenant Colonel Wood commanded the sixteen-person unit). For "Security Support Team" moniker, see Wood statement and AFRICOM and SOCAFRICA Briefing, p. 78.

[41] AFRICOM and SOCAFRICA Briefing, pp. 13-15, 58-59. For General Demspey's understanding of these events, see Dempsey Briefing, p. 9. Mr. Reid and Major General Roberson repeated this assessment and said that the SST was withdrawn at Ambassador Stevens' behest. (See May Benghazi Briefing, Part II, pp. 40, 47.) The Interim Progress Report makes clear that Tripoli embassy staff sought additional security through established bureaucratic channels but once higher authority at the State Department rejected this request, Ambassador Stevens was obligated to accept the decision. (See Interim Progress Report pp. 7-9; and Gregory N. Hicks, "Benghazi and the Smearing of Chris Stevens," *Wall Street Journal,* January 22, 2014.) At a Senate Homeland Security and Governmental Affairs subcommittee hearing in July 2013, Patrick Kennedy, the Under Secretary of State for Management, was asked "[d]id you at any time communicate or confirm to the Defense Department that the State Department would not be needing the SST after August 2012?" He answered "I did." (See Hearing Transcript, U.S. Senate, Committee on Homeland Security and Governmental Affairs, Subcommittee on Financial and Contracting Oversight, "Implementation of Wartime Contracting Reforms," July 16, 2013, p. 31.) In contrast, Gregory Hicks, the Deputy Chief of Mission in Libya, told the U.S. Senate's Select Intelligence Committee that DOD shared the Department of State's interest in changing the mission of the SST unit ("DOD wanted to change the nature of the SST team as much as State wanted it changed;" see Review of the Terrorist Attacks, p. 20.) Separately he has written that DOD was eager to limit the SST size until the Libyan government granted its members diplomatic immunity. (See Hicks, "Benghazi and the Smearing of Chris Stevens.,") For a discussion of Ambassador Steven's consideration of various DOD security capabilities and the final arrangements, see Briefing Transcript (redacted), U.S. House of

In a written exchange with the committee, General Ham said that he could "state with certainty" that after the SST drawdown, AFRICOM "did not receive any direction to provide U.S. military forces to augment security for U.S. personnel in Libya."[42] In separate correspondence, Vice Admiral Kurt Tidd, the Director for Operations for the Joint Staff (J-3), echoed this point. He declared that "[f]ollowing August 3, 2012, when the Defense Department Site Security Team completed its mission in Libya, until September 11, 2012, neither I nor anyone in my directorate received requests for additional U.S. military forces to augment security for U.S. personnel in Libya."[43]

Committee briefers emphasized that between the time that Muammar Gaddafi was deposed and the Benghazi attack, the Department of Defense provided "everything the State Department asked for from the DOD."[44] General Dempsey said something similar to the Senate.[45] Based upon the briefings, staff interviews, and written materials, majority members believe that DOD persistently acceded to State Department requests, while also supporting that department's efforts to establish arrangements in Libya that more closely resembled those typically found in other diplomatic posts. Thus, rather than continuing to assign a Site Security Team indefinitely, DOD believed that the State Department would beef up its own diplomatic security forces, request the assignment of a Marine security guard detachment, or work with DOD to develop some other long-term solution.[46]

Representatives, Committee on Armed Services, Subcommittee on Oversight and Investigations, "Briefing on Benghazi," July 31, 2013, pp. 12-13 (hereafter "July Benghazi Briefing").

[42] General Carter F. Ham, Commander, U.S. Africa Command, letter to Howard P. "Buck" McKeon, Chairman, Committee on Armed Services, October 31, 2012.

[43] Vice Admiral Kurt W. Tidd, Director for Operations, Joint Staff, letter to Howard P. "Buck" McKeon, Chairman, Committee on Armed Services, October 29, 2012.

[44] May Benghazi Briefing, Part I, p. 66. Similarly, Major General Roberson was asked to confirm that "[t]o the best of your knowledge, there was nothing" needed for the security of State Department activities "that State Department asked for that [DOD] denied" in the period "prior to the attack." Major General Roberson replied, "[t]hat is correct." (See May Benghazi Briefing, Part I, p. 81.)

[45] Senate Hearing, pp. 29-30, 49-50, 72-73.

[46] See, e.g., Hearing Transcript, U.S. House of Representatives, Committee on Armed Services, Subcommittee on Oversight and Investigations, "the Defense Department's Posture for September 11, 2013: What are the Lessons of Benghazi?" September 19, 2013, p. 32 (hereafter "September Lessons Learned Hearing"); Dempsey Briefing, pp. 11, 14; Review of the Terrorist Attacks, p 20; and unclassified portions of email, Lieutenant General Robert B. Neller, Director for Operations, Joint Staff, to Patrick Kennedy, Under Secretary of State for Management, July 11, 2012 (in committee possession). For references to discussions within DOD about the possibility of sending additional forces without a State Department request, see Dempsey Briefing, pp. 9-13. The absence of a recommendation from DOD commanders for additional forces is noted in Vice Admiral Tidd letter to Chairman McKeon; General Ham letter to Chairman McKeon; and AFRICOM and SOCAFRICA Briefing, pp. 10-11, 27. Furthermore, in correspondence with the committee, Admiral William H. McRaven, the commander of U.S. Special Operations Command (USSOCOM), wrote that no one in his command recommended "deployment of additional U.S. military forces to Libya" before September 11, 2012. (See Admiral William H. McRaven, Commander, U.S. Special Operations Command, letter to Howard P. "Buck" McKeon, Chairman, Committee on Armed Services, October 25, 2012.) This letter also stipulates "USSOCOM does not make independent recommendations for any additional forces—USSOCOM is positioned to support requests that would come from USAFRICOM. . . . USSOCOM did not receive any request from USAFRICOM for additional forces."

III. Defense Department officials believed nearly from the outset of violence in Benghazi that it was a terrorist attack rather than a protest gone awry, and the President subsequently permitted the military to respond with minimal direction.

Shortly after the Benghazi attack began, General Ham, who was coincidentally visiting the Pentagon from AFRICOM headquarters in Germany, was informed. He was told the SMC was under fire and the location of Ambassador Stevens and a State Department colleague was unknown. General Ham then personally provided this information to General Dempsey and both then "immediately" briefed Secretary Panetta.[47]

Secretary Panetta and General Dempsey then left for the White House to attend an unrelated routine weekly meeting with the President. Upon arrival, the two discussed the attack with the President for fifteen to thirty minutes, at which time they presumably shared all that was known about the unfolding events, including the fact that the ambassador and the subordinate (Mr. Sean Smith) were missing.[48] According to Secretary Panetta's statements to the Senate, the President "directed both myself and General Dempsey to do everything we need to do to try to protect the lives" in Benghazi.[49] General Dempsey recounted to the House Armed Services Committee:

> the President instructed us to use all available assets to respond to the attacks to ensure the safety of U.S. personnel in Libya and to protect U.S. personnel and interests throughout the region.[50]

Secretary Panetta and General Dempsey eventually returned to the Pentagon and guided the response from there.[51]

"[A]s to specifics" of the U.S. reaction, Secretary Panetta testified to the Senate that the President "left that up to us." Secretary Panetta said the President was "well informed" about events and worried about American lives. He and General Dempsey also testified they had no further contact with the President, nor did Secretary of State Hillary Clinton ever communicate with them that evening.[52]

Both the secretary and General Dempsey did make clear to SASC that staff members at the Pentagon and White House were in touch at this time. General Dempsey said the President's "staff was engaged with the National Military Command Center pretty constantly through the

---

[47] AFRICOM and SOCAFRICA Briefing, p. 35, 37-38, and Aspen Remarks.

[48] May Benghazi Briefing, Part II, p. 50-52; AFRICOM and SOCAFRICA Briefing, p. 38, Dempsey Briefing, p. 6; Senate Hearing, pp. 15-16, 35, 45.

[49] Senate Hearing, p. 31.

[50] Dempsey Briefing, p. 6.

[51] AFRICOM and SOCAFRICA Briefing, p. 71.

[52] Senate Hearing, pp. 31-32, 35, 38, 46, and 70. Secretary Clinton testified before the Senate Foreign Relations Committee in January 2013 that she and General Dempsey spoke about the attack on September 12. Furthermore, she said on the day of the attack she participated in a "secure video conference" which included "senior officials" from DOD. See Hearing Transcript, U.S. Senate, Committee on Foreign Relations, "Senate Foreign Relations Committee Holds Hearing on Terrorist Attacks in Benghazi, Libya," January 23, 2013, *CQ Congressional Transcripts,* pp. 9.

period."[53] Nevertheless, these staffers appear to have placed no limitations on the military's immediate reaction to the attack. General Dempsey answered "no" when asked by the House Armed Services Committee if he had "any restrictions placed on whatever it is that you thought needed to get done to respond to . . . Benghazi."[54]

Terrorist attack discerned at outset

General Ham and others also reported to the committee that they readily believed the events in Benghazi to be an attack, not a protest against a YouTube video that had spun out of control. "It became pretty apparent to me, and I think to most at Africa Command pretty shortly after this attack began, that this was an attack," General Ham said, although he also suggested that in his meeting with Secretary Panetta and General Dempsey there was some "peripheral" consideration about the underlying cause.[55] "[I]initially it was somewhat uncertain to me," he said. "But as the events unfolded," and he learned from those on the ground about the enemy use of "rocket-propelled grenade[s]" and "pretty well aimed small arms fire" he said "it started to become pretty clear that this was certainly a terrorist attack and not just—not something sporadic."[56] He said he conveyed this assessment to Secretary Panetta and General Dempsey.[57]

U.S. Marine Colonel George H. Bristol, who was the commander of Joint Special Operations Task Force – Trans Sahara in September 2012 and thus in communication with U.S. military personnel at the U.S. embassy in Tripoli, also briefed the committee. When he was asked, "did anyone in the military or anyone surrounding this event ever call [the events in Benghazi] anything but an attack?" he replied, "[n]ot that I remember." To the specific question, in "any of the informal discussion[s] that you were a part of or had the ability to hear about, did anyone call this a demonstration that got out of control?" he answered "No."[58]

In light of the prevalence, certainty, and immediacy of assessments within DOD about the nature of the attack and the fact that the military did not condition its response on the assumptions that it had been sparked by a protest, it seems clear that contrasting descriptions did not originate with Defense officials most familiar with the events in Benghazi. Majority members believe it is essential that precise, accurate information is conveyed to every level of command in the event of emergencies such as this. Furthermore, subject to appropriate classification restrictions, these same standards must be reflected in the information released to the public.

IV. The U.S. military's response to the Benghazi attack was severely degraded because of the location and readiness posture of U.S. forces, and because of lack of clarity about how the terrorist action was unfolding. However, given the uncertainty about the prospective

---

[53] Senate Hearing, pp. 32 (quote), 66.

[54] Dempsey Briefing, p. 14.

[55] AFRICOM and SOCAFRICA Briefing, p. 38. General Ham also said, "I think . . . there was some preliminary discussion about . . . maybe there was a demonstration. But . . . personally . . . I think the [U.S. Africa] command very quickly got to the point [of believing] this was not a demonstration, this was a terrorist attack." (See AFRICOM and SOCAFRICA Briefing, p. 50.)

[56] AFRICOM and SOCAFRICA Briefing, pp. 48-49. See also Aspen Remarks.

[57] AFRICOM and SOCAFRICA Briefing, p. 50.

[58] July Benghazi Briefing, pp. 50-51.

length and scope of the attack, military commanders did not take all possible steps to prepare for a more extended operation.

When the Department of State learned the SMC was being assaulted on September 11, officials notified DOD's National Military Command Center at the Pentagon.[59] Thus began a chain of events that involved DOD allocating various forces to the crisis. The response decisions were based upon what forces were available and could readily be brought to bear on the situation as it was understood by senior leaders.

The first step DOD took upon learning of the attack involved a U.S. drone that was overflying Darnah, a city in northeastern Libya. AFRICOM's operations officer immediately redirected the unarmed Predator to Benghazi, which was about an hour's flight time away.[60] Separately, following the meeting in the White House, Secretary Panetta (in consultation with General Ham, General Dempsey, and others) verbally authorized three specific actions. First, two Marine FAST platoons in Rota, Spain were ordered to prepare to deploy; one bound for Benghazi and one destined for Tripoli. Second, a special operations unit assigned to the European Command, known as a Commander's In-Extremis Force (CIF), which was training in Croatia was ordered to move to a U.S. Naval Air Station in Sigonella, Italy and await further instructions. Third, a special operations unit in the United States was also dispatched to the region.[61] These orders were issued approximately two to four hours after the initial attack on the SMC.[62]

Impossibility of preparing for all scenarios

Majority members believe the regional and global force posture assumed by the military on September 11, 2012 limited the response. Majority members recognize, of course, that it is impossible for the Department of Defense to have adequate forces prepared to respond immediately to every conceivable global contingency. Ensuring that preparations exist for some likely possibilities is not to be confused with the ability to anticipate all prospective circumstances, especially in highly volatile regions.[63]

---

[59] AFRICOM and SOCAFRICA Briefing, p. 37.

[60] May Benghazi Briefing, Part I, p. 54 (quote); AFRICOM and SOCAFRICA Briefing, pp. 34-36, 46; Aspen Remarks; ARB Report, pp. 25, 37; and "Timeline of Department of Defense Actions on September 11-12, 2012," attached to Elizabeth King, Assistant Secretary of Defense (Legislative Affairs) letter to Howard P. "Buck" McKeon, Chairman, Committee on Armed Services, May 1, 2013 (hereafter "DOD timeline). About six hours later, another drone replaced the first. See Ibid.

[61] Dempsey Briefing, p. 6; DOD timeline; ARB Report, p. 37; Senate Hearing, p. 9; Aspen Remarks; and Elizabeth King, Assistant Secretary of Defense (Legislative Affairs) letter to Elijah E. Cummings, Ranking Member, Committee on Oversight and Government Reform, May 7, 2013. For the specific delineation of DOD's total response actions, the FAST platoons, the CIF, and a U.S.-based unit (and the exclusion of fighter aircraft from this list), see May Benghazi Briefing, Part I, pp. 74-76.

[62] DoD timeline.

[63] For example, Major General Roberson remarked to the committee, "[w]e don't have assets to respond like a fire call[; to] jump down the pole and respond for any American that is under fire anywhere in the world." Similarly, Mr. Reid observed: "it is tough to get there [i.e. a trouble spot] within a few hours no matter how alert you are," and DOD should not be considered "an emergency response force that needs to be there within single digit hours because it is just frankly not that practical," nor an acceptable "planning model." (See May Benghazi Briefing, Part I, pp. 34, 36, 43.) On the "tremendous resource implications" of a notional "Department of Defense capability to

Majority members acknowledge that embassy security involves estimating and managing risk. Department representatives appearing before the committee pointed out that some danger will always be present, regardless of the preparations, especially in tension-prone areas of the world.[64] Before the Benghazi attacks, there was also the presumption (in Libya and elsewhere) that indigenous forces would be more helpful in protecting Americans than proved to be the case.[65]

Given the military's preparations on September 11, 2012, majority members have not yet discerned any response alternatives that could have likely changed the outcome of the Benghazi attack. While majority members are reluctant to disagree with specific tactical decisions made by professional career uniformed officers in the heat of battle and they believe the U.S. military performed well in responding to the attacks, it is nonetheless necessary to evaluate thoroughly the choices commanders made.

Limitations on situational awareness

Majority members also believe that the military response may have been complicated by the lack of much real-time knowledge of what was transpiring on the ground. The dearth of information seems relevant when considering how commanders shaped their response to the attack. For example, about 20 minutes after the attack started, CIA security personnel from a nearby CIA facility (informally known as "the annex") raced to the SMC. Once there, CIA personnel exchanged fire with the attackers and then, joined by the SMC survivors, fought their way back to the annex. Amidst sporadic fire, that facility then took two discrete attacks, including a mortar barrage that killed CIA security personnel Tyrone Woods and Glen Doherty.[66]

Significantly, however, DOD reported to the committee that General Ham and some others at AFRICOM did not know the annex existed before the attack on the SMC began.[67] Learning about a second facility in Benghazi amidst an attack may have complicated the military's process of assessing events and response options, in part because the second location was both an attack target and a U.S. security resource. Although the committee will continue to explore this point, majority members believe a combatant commander's apparent unfamiliarity with a vital detail in his Area of Responsibility further illustrates the deficiency of the review undertaken by the White House before September 11, 2012.

In addition, briefers reported that those attempting to respond to or assess the Benghazi attacks often used cell phones to communicate.[68] Obviously, that communication technique in a location with an underdeveloped telecommunications infrastructure poses difficulties. Further,

---

respond to any U.S. diplomatic facility within a specified period of time," see General Carter Ham statement in AFRICOM and SOCAFRICA Briefing, p. 47; and Aspen Remarks.

[64] May Benghazi Briefing, Part II, p. 60.

[65] May Benghazi Briefing, Part I, p. 36. For General Ham's endorsement of increasing the capabilities of indigenous forces, see AFRICOM and SOCAFRICA Briefing, p. 62.

[66] Review of the Terrorist Attacks, pp. 4-9.

[67] Unclassified information captioned "Questions" provided by the Department of Defense (in committee possession). This information also notes "it is possible other DoD assets in country may have known."

[68] AFRICOM and SOCAFRICA Briefing, pp. 48, 81, 89, 154; and July Benghazi Briefing, p. 13-14.

the Predator drone could not provide complete and contextualized awareness of events.[69] As the committee was told, the first drone (and one that replaced it later) was able to provide information to "rear headquarters," but personnel there believed the data was insufficient to guide the development of "operational judgments."[70]

Committee staff and some Members of Congress have reviewed a classified recording of the video that the drones transmitted to operators at a very distant location during the attack. This review allowed an opportunity to assess the situational awareness provided by the drones and the difficulty of using the information provided for tactical decision-making.

Armed Drones or Manned Aircraft

The Department of Defense had no armed drones or manned aircraft prepared for combat readily available and nearby on September 11. Secretary Panetta told the Senate in February 2013 that armed Unmanned Aerial Vehicles (UAVs), AC-130 ground attack gunships, or other similar planes "were not in the vicinity."[71] Mr. Reid echoed this to the House Armed Services Committee in May 2013 when he declared "[g]iven the time and distance factors involved, dispatching an armed aircraft to Benghazi was not an option available to us at the time."[72]

As the result of a specific request from the committee, DOD accounted for the location of each of its AC-130 aircraft in the military's inventory. DOD reported to the committee that no AC-130s were in the region in the days before the Benghazi attack, including for maintenance, crew rest, or merely transiting through the area. However, DOD also reported to the committee that some of these planes were deployed to "southern Europe" on September 14, in order "to support operations in North Africa."[73]

Similarly, the U.S. Air Force F-16 fighters stationed at Aviano, Italy at the time were configured for training flights.[74] None were on combat alert.[75] Furthermore, unlike typical preparations during the Cold War, NATO allies also had no planes on war-fighting status. This meant other nations could not offer combat aircraft to respond on behalf of the United States.[76]

---

[69] Aspen Remarks and ARB Report, p. 37.

[70] May Benghazi Briefing, Part I, p. 54 (quote); AFRICOM and SOCAFRICA Briefing, pp. 45-46; Aspen Remarks; and DOD timeline, pp. 25, 27. However, the CIA believes the drone was a "critical resource" which gave its personnel in Tripoli and Benghazi "situation awareness" as events unfolded. (See Review of the Terrorist Attacks, p. 32.)

[71] Senate Hearing, p. 9.

[72] May Benghazi Briefing, Part I, p. 16.

[73] Unclassified information captioned "AC-130's" (in committee possession). In 2012, a Defense Department spokesman also publically declared that "no AC-130 was within a continent's range of Benghazi" the night of the attack. (See Ken Dilanian, "U.S. officials counter criticism in Benghazi attack," *Los Angeles Times*, November 2, 2012.)

[74] May Benghazi Briefing, Part I, pp. 32, 34.

[75] May Benghazi Briefing, Part I, p. 75.

[76] May Benghazi Briefing, Part I, pp. 80-81. Indeed, to the extent that NATO air force units are prepared to take any action they often must rely on the United States. For example, in the course of the 2011 NATO air operations conducted during the Libyan uprising, one reliable source describes the treaty organization as being "highly dependent" on the U.S. Air Force which was "a key enabler" of the strikes. See John A. Tirpak, "Lessons From Libya," *Air Force Magazine*, December 2011.

In considering possible threats in the AFRICOM region before the Benghazi attack, General Ham told the committee he personally dismissed the prospect of requesting a higher alert status or repositioning some U.S. F-16s. This is because he doubted their utility to any threat his command might face on September 11.[77] Even after the attack started, General Ham and others in the Department discounted the possibility of beginning the process to arm and dispatch one or more of these fighters. Officials also worried about the presence of shoulder-fired Surface-to-Air missiles in Libya, the difficulty of vectoring any planes safely over the desired location, and the challenge of distinguishing friend from foe on the ground.[78]

Military leaders apparently believed that in the time needed to recall aircrews, and reconfigure planes from training to combat status, the events in Benghazi would have subsided. As Major General Roberson explained in a briefing to the U.S. Senate's Select Committee on Intelligence, sending a plane from Aviano would have required assembling munitions for the aircraft and then the military would need to "load weapons, get tankers to support it, and get [the fighter] there [to Benghazi]. There was no way that we were going to be able to do that."[79]

As General Roberson described, it would have taken a long time to prepare aircraft and make aerial fueling arrangements so planes would have sufficient range to fly to Benghazi, loiter overhead, and then return to base. From their other responsibilities in overseeing DOD and from consultations with a recently-retired fighter pilot well acquainted with such matters, majority members are aware of many other complex elements that must have been considered before deciding (or not) to deploy planes for combat. For example, they must be equipped with countermeasures to defend against antiaircraft weapons and radar-equipped control aircraft (commonly known as AWACS), and search and rescue crews also typically need to be positioned in the area. Furthermore, it is necessary to have communications with friendly forces on the ground to ensure proper targeting.

Of course, when the attack on the SMC commenced, the eventual nature and scope of the events was unknown. Although Americans in Benghazi were under fire for much of a seven and one-half hour period, the storming of the SMC could have been the start of an even longer engagement or a siege, or been part of a hostage taking effort or a broader coordinated attack

---

[77] AFRICOM and SOCAFRICA Briefing, pp. 53, 64, 67-68.

[78] May Benghazi Briefing, Part I, pp. 23-25, 75, 85; AFRICOM and SOCAFRICA Briefing, p. 46; and Senate Hearing, p. 9. A year before the attack, the authoritative publication reported that there were as many as 20,000 man-portable surface-to-air missiles in Libya, including advanced Russian IGLA-S weapons (known in the West by the designation SA-24). (See "After Ghadaffi-Libya enters a new era," *IHS Jane's Defence Weekly*, September 16, 2011; and "Russia moots UN resolution to secure Libyan stockpiles," *IHS Jane's Defence Weekly*, October 27, 2011.)

[79] Review of the Terrorist Attacks, pp. 28-29. In this same colloquy with the Senate committee, Major General Roberson is quoted as saying "[t]he assets that we had available were [F-15E] Strike Eagles loaded with live weapons that could have responded, but they were located in Djibouti, which is the equivalent of the distance between here [Washington D.C.] and Los Angeles." (See Review of the Terrorist Attacks, p. 28) The wording of this quotation suggests a greater response capability than actually existed. Based upon information provided to the committee by DOD, readily dispatching these aircraft was not feasible, in part because it would have taken at least 28 hours to stage tankers and make other necessary preparations for the 4.5 to six hour flight. (See information in committee possession.)

across Libya or elsewhere.[80] Although given their location and readiness status it was not possible to dispatch armed aircraft before survivors left Benghazi, the committee will continue to evaluate why DOD found it unnecessary to begin to prepare fighters and make other arrangements, especially in light of the concern that the hostilities could spread to Tripoli.[81]

Unarmed Overflight

As for scrambling an unarmed fighter jet, Major General Roberson, a veteran F-16 pilot, discussed the theoretical possibility of such an overflight with the committee.

> [T]here is a potential you could have flown a show of force and made everyone aware there was a fighter airborne. Would it have changed anything? Certainly, we couldn't have gotten there before the ambassador [and a State Department colleague were] dead. We know that. But even if we had gotten there before the annex attack [which killed two more Americans] in my experience it [would not] necessarily stop the fighting, especially if [the enemy were] conditioned to it.[82]

This is because, he explained, "experienced" combatants can discern "show of force" overflights from aerial attacks and react accordingly. "[T]hey know what it means. It means there [are] no bombs dropping. It just means you are trying to let them know you are there." He concluded, "I can't tell" if an unarmed overflight would have "been effective or not in Benghazi."[83]

In recounting his experiences to the Committee on Oversight and Government Reform, Mr. Greg Hicks, who was the Deputy Chief of Mission (DCM) in Tripoli and became the senior U.S. diplomat in Libya once Ambassador Stevens was missing, suggested that he thought such an aircraft from Aviano might arrive over Benghazi within a few hours.[84] Mr. Hicks thought an unarmed overflight was desirable. Using a colloquialism for a fighter, he declared before the Oversight Committee that "a fast mover flying over Benghazi at some point . . . as soon as possible, might very well have prevented some of the bad things that happened that night."[85]

---

[80] For an account of fighting over nearly eight hours, see Review of the Terrorist Attacks.

[81] Similarly, there is some question why a C-17 was ordered to prepare to deploy to Libya about eight hours after the attack started and then took another eight hours to get airborne. See DOD timeline. In connection with this and other issues, committee staff has also reviewed a classified attack timeline made available to the committee by DOD. Majority members note that evaluation of the timeline has been made more difficult by the fact that the Department has refused to provide a copy for the committee's retention on the grounds that it is a draft compiled only for internal use. (See Howard P. "Buck" McKeon, Chairman, Committee on Armed Services letter to Elizabeth King, Assistant Secretary of Defense (Legislative Affairs) April 17, 2013; and Assistant Secretary Elizabeth King letter to Chairman McKeon, May 1, 2013.)

[82] May Benghazi Briefing, Part I, p. 85.

[83] May Benghazi Briefing, Part I, p. 85.

[84] Oversight Hearing, pp. 11, 14. For the SST leader's account of this subject, see AFRICOM and SOCAFRICA Briefing, p. 100.

[85] Oversight Hearing, p. 13. At least one news story has also asserted that an individual in Benghazi who was associated with the Central Intelligence Agency "repeatedly" requested assistance from "combat aircraft" but a CIA superior "ignored" the demand because "he knew that no combat aircraft were available for such a mission." (See Kimberly Dozier, "CIA Benghazi Team Clash Led to 'Stand Down' Report," Associated Press, December 14, 2013.)

Although the committee will continue to gather and assess information on this topic, it seems that had the risks been deemed acceptable and one or more unarmed fighter aircraft were flown over Benghazi, the effort would probably have been ineffective. Even if such planes could have been dispatched in a timely manner, it would have been extraordinarily difficult for pilots (even with night vision capability) to identify and overfly attackers in very low light. Furthermore, to minimize the antiaircraft threat, an overflight would probably taken place at a relatively high altitude and this would have lessened the putative deterrent effect on enemy forces arrayed far below.[86] This is especially the case because the Benghazi attackers demonstrated that they were the sort of experienced fighters that Major General Roberson warned might be less fearful of an unarmed overflight. Those who struck the U.S. facilities seemed to have carefully planned their actions, scouted the scene beforehand, and were able to skillfully and accurately employ mortar fire.[87]

Nonetheless, some have suggested that dispatching unarmed aircraft should have been considered, at least as an interim step before more about the attack and potential response became known. In this reading, had one or more jets been launched, a recall order could have been issued before arriving over Benghazi if problems arose with refueling or overflight permissions, or if a preferable alternative was developed in the meantime. But, in light of all these factors, majority members believe the use of unarmed aircraft, with no countermeasure capability, refueling arrangements, or targeting assistance, amidst a dangerous antiaircraft environment, would have offered only a small likelihood of benefitting those under attack. It makes sense that this remote option was apparently not more actively contemplated.

Ground Forces

As for the two FAST platoons, the CIF, and the special operations unit in the U.S., the posture of each meant they needed as much as six hours preparation before departing for Libya and they then had to travel varying distances of considerable length.[88] The attacks in Benghazi were over within approximately seven and one-half hours, before any of these units arrived. In the case of the CIF, the Department of Defense declared in correspondence to Congress that "the time requirements for notification, load, and transit . . . prevented the CIF from being at [Benghazi] in time . . . to change events," despite the fact that the upon being alerted the team "immediately began to fulfill its tasking" and moved to "an intermediate staging location."[89] The committee, however, will continue to examine the fact that DOD's posture allowed the CIF to be training on September 11.

---

[86] These dangers are especially apt in light of the fact that a U.S. fighter crashed outside Benghazi a year before while enforcing the no-fly zone during the anti-government uprising. See Tirpak, "Lessons From Libya," p. 37; and Rob Crilly, James Kirkup, and Rob Winnett, "Libya: US fighter jet crash lands in field near Benghazi," *Telegraph*, March 22, 2011.

[87] For references to accurate mortar fire and deliberate and organized (if not necessarily extensively planned) attacks, see Review of the Terrorist Attacks, pp. 9, 24-25.

[88] Senate Hearing, p. 45, Aspen Remarks. Some alterations in the response of ground units were also made mid-course because the Department of Defense initially thought Ambassador Stevens may have been kidnapped, thus potentially necessitating hostage rescue capabilities. (See Senate Hearing, p. 59.)

[89] Assistant Secretary King to Ranking Member Cummings.

As far as the Marines are concerned, according to General Dempsey, once one FAST platoon was underway it also stopped at a "forward-basing location" so that the Marines could don civilian clothes. This was apparently done upon the request of the Libyan government, conveyed by the Department of State.[90] Presumably, warfighters changed out of uniform because of concerns that the arrival of combat-ready troops might unduly alarm or inflame Libyan observers.

Although General Dempsey acknowledged to the Senate that this action delayed the platoon's arrival in Libya, he said it was not enough to prevent it from getting to Benghazi before attack survivors departed.[91] In sum, "[o]nce we started moving forces," General Dempsey told the Senate, "nothing stopped us, nothing slowed us."[92] However, at least in the case of the FAST platoon, there seem to have been some challenges in proceeding expeditiously.

About seventeen hours after Secretary Panetta ordered ground forces to prepare to deploy, the CIF had only made it as far as "an intermediate staging base in southern Europe." An hour later, one FAST platoon arrived in Tripoli. Despite having travelled across the globe, the special operations force from the U.S. arrived in Europe about thirty minutes later.[93] Majority members remain concerned about these response times and will continue to seek all necessary information to understand and place in context this timing.

V. There was no "stand down" order issued to U.S. military personnel in Tripoli who sought to join the fight in Benghazi. However, because official reviews after the attack were not sufficiently comprehensive, there was confusion about the roles and responsibilities of these individuals.

After the Benghazi attack began, six U.S. security personnel left the embassy in Tripoli on a chartered Libyan aircraft to lend assistance.[94] Two of these individuals were U.S. soldiers on a specialized assignment who took orders in such circumstances from authorities outside of AFRICOM and Special Operations Command-Africa (SOCAFRICA).[95] These were the only U.S. military personnel who got to Benghazi before survivors arrived in Tripoli on a chartered plane, and they performed heroically.

Four other military personnel remained behind in Tripoli. They comprised the reduced and revamped Security Support Team and were assigned to AFRICOM.[96] Army Lieutenant Colonel S.E. Gibson, who led the reconfigured SST, told the committee that when he learned of the attack in Benghazi "[t]here were concerns this might be part of a larger coordinated attack . .

---

[90] Senate Hearing pp. 71-72.

[91] Dempsey Briefing, p. 41; and Senate Hearing, pp. 71-72. The Benghazi-bound Marines were subsequently diverted to Tripoli. See ibid.

[92] Senate Hearing, p. 59.

[93] DOD timeline.

[94] ARB Report, p. 25; May Benghazi Briefing, Part I, p. 47. The number of individuals in this effort is reported as seven in the ARB Report, pp. 25, 27; May Benghazi Briefing, Part I, p. 77; and May Benghazi Briefing, Part II, p. 24; but six in the DOD timeline. The discrepancy is apparently traced to the fact that one of the seven was "a linguist" and presumably a Libyan national. See Review of the Terrorist Attacks, p. 29.

[95] AFRICOM and SOCAFRICA Briefing, pp. 125-126.

[96] DOD timeline; AFRICOM and SOCAFRICA Briefing, pp. 54, 78-82, 95, 125-127.

. with the U.S. Embassy [in] Tripoli being targeted."[97] Indeed, Colonel George Bristol of the Joint Special Operations Task Force – Trans Sahara briefed the committee that he told Lieutenant Colonel Gibson in a quick telephone call from another country in Africa "that the U.S. embassy in Tripoli was his priority" and he must "ensure that it was protected."[98] Therefore, because of concern about the possibility of a follow-on attack in Tripoli, the four SST soldiers, including a medic, joined "less than a handful" of State Department security personnel in helping to safeguard embassy staff and facilities.[99]

However, after the diplomatic staff had been moved to what Lieutenant Colonel Gibson considered a "secure" location in Tripoli, he informed AFRICOM that he was about to take his three special operators to Benghazi on a Libyan transport plane. At that time, Rear Admiral Brian L. Losey, SOCAFRICA's commander, conveyed an order to Lieutenant Colonel Gibson to remain in Tripoli to defend Americans there.[100] Rear Admiral Losey said he was concerned about the possibility of follow-on attacks in Tripoli or a potential for attempts at hostage taking.[101] Preferring to move, however, Lieutenant Colonel Gibson told the committee he was "visibly upset" at the time.[102] But, Rear Admiral Losey explained to the committee that it was rooted in his belief that Lieutenant Colonel Gibson's team was "the only military element . . . in Tripoli that had any security experience whatsoever" and "it seemed prudent" to divide the few military personnel in Libya between Tripoli and Benghazi rather than concentrate them in one location.[103] He said his decision was based on consultation with two other officers and the three had "about 90 years of collective Special Operations experience" between them.[104]

Mr. Hicks, the DCM, described Lieutenant Colonel Gibson's distress to the Committee on Oversight and Government Reform in May 2013 and he did not object during the hearing when the soldier's instructions were categorized as orders to "stand down." This led some to conclude erroneously that inaction rather than an alternative warfighting posture was ordered for Lieutenant Colonel Gibson's four men.[105] But, Lieutenant Colonel Gibson's instructions were precisely clarified in a colloquy before the Armed Services Committee:

---

[97] AFRICOM and SOCAFRICA Briefing, p. 80.

[98] July Benghazi Briefing, p. 14.

[99] May Benghazi Briefing, Part I, p. 48; May Benghazi Briefing, Part II, p. 39; AFRICOM and SOCAFRICA Briefing, pp. 29-32, 44, 80-82, 84-85, 88-89, 91 and 97 (quotation), 105; and Oversight Hearing, pp. 11-12.

[100] AFRICOM and SOCAFRICA Briefing, pp. 82-83, 88-89, 92-93, and 105-106. In seeking to go to Benghazi, the team intended to help protect the airport there, presumably to safeguard it for evacuating Americans. (See AFRICOM and SOCAFRICA Briefing, p. 106.) After Lieutenant Colonel Gibson learned the survivors from the Benghazi attack had boarded a Libyan plane and were flying to the Tripoli airport, Lieutenant Colonel Gibson requested permission from AFRICOM to leave his location and meet the inbound aircraft. Again, he was ordered to stay in place with the diplomatic personnel. Lieutenant Colonel Gibson told the committee he was "vocal in my disagreement with this directive" and about five minutes later AFRICOM permitted his group to proceed to the airport. (See AFRICOM and SOCAFRICA Briefing, pp. 84, 92-93.)

[101] AFRICOM and SOCAFRICA Briefing, p. 128.

[102] AFRICOM and SOCAFRICA Briefing, p. 83, 89, 99.

[103] AFRICOM and SOCAFRICA Briefing, pp.83 (Gibson quotation), 105-106 (Losey quotation), 111 (Losey quotation), and 113.

[104] AFRICOM and SOCAFRICA Briefing, p. 105.

[105] AFRICOM and SOCAFRICA Briefing, p. 87; and Oversight Hearing, pp. 12-13. The response of the CIA personnel at the annex has also been critiqued. Some discern an unrelated "stand down" or delay with this group. (See Dozier, "CIA Benghazi Team Clash Led to 'Stand Down' Report.") This issue appears to be settled in Review of the Terrorist Attacks, pp. 4-5.

Mrs. Roby: . . . Do you agree that you and your team were ordered to . . . "stand down?"

Colonel Gibson: Madam Chairman, I was not ordered to stand down. I was ordered to remain in place. "Stand down" implies that we cease all operations, cease all activities. We continued to support the team that was in Tripoli. We continued to maintain visibility of the events as they unfolded.[106]

Lieutenant Colonel Gibson made it clear to the committee that "in hindsight" he believes remaining in Tripoli was appropriate. "The decision by my higher headquarters to not get on that plane [to Benghazi] was the correct decision," he told the committee.[107] Indeed, he noted that had his unit left Tripoli as he originally intended, the medic would not have been available to treat the wounded when they arrived there later from Benghazi.[108]

As Lieutenant Colonel Gibson noted to the committee, there is no doubt the instructions to remain in Tripoli to assist in protecting embassy staff was a "legal and lawful" order with which he properly complied.[109] Rear Admiral Losey recounted that Lieutenant Colonel Gibson lodged no objections with him.[110] Although not directed to "stand down," some might believe nonetheless that Lieutenant Colonel Gibson should have been allowed to proceed to Benghazi. But Lieutenant Colonel Gibson's orders rested upon the impressions that Rear Admiral Losey and other more senior officers had of the threat in Libya, the adequacy of the defenses that the State Department personnel and local forces could provide, and how best to deploy and utilize the SST.

If DOD intended for the actions undertaken by Lieutenant Colonel Gibson and his team, and their chain of command's management of the situation to be incorporated into the department's lessons learned, the department undertook inadequate follow-up on these topics. It appears that until Congressional oversight of the Benghazi response began, many senior officials in DOD were unclear about the SST's activities on the day of the attack, orders the team leader had been given, the reasons apparently underlying them, and his desire at one point for alternative instructions. General Ham told the committee that, while he agreed with the order to Lieutenant Colonel Gibson to remain in Tripoli, he did not know about it until Mr. Hicks' testimony.[111] General Dempsey said something similar.[112] A DOD spokesman also separately admitted that before "news reports" about the four personnel, many "officials . . . were unaware

---

[106] AFRICOM and SOCAFRICA Briefing, pp. 87. Similarly, in a Senate Budget Committee hearing, General Dempsey declared of the four soldiers: "They weren't told to stand down. A stand down means don't do anything. They were told . . . that the mission they were asked to perform was not in Benghazi, but was at Tripoli airport." (See Senate Budget Hearing, p. 34.)

[107] AFRICOM and SOCAFRICA Briefing, p. 88.

[108] AFRICOM and SOCAFRICA Briefing, p. 85.

[109] AFRICOM and SOCAFRICA Briefing, p. 85.

[110] AFRICOM and SOCAFRICA Briefing, pp. 108, 112-113.

[111] AFRICOM and SOCAFRICA Briefing, pp. 30-31, 59.

[112] Dempsey Briefing, pp. 35-36.

of instructions" issued to the SST.[113] Although the Department subsequently released information that is generally in accord with what participants later recounted to the committee, the initial inattention to these issues suggests a failure to consider fully how best to improve decision making in future crisis situations involving Defense personnel engaged in diplomatic security activities.[114]

Furthermore, what transpired with the SST also may not have been considered by the five members and six staffers of Department of State's Accountability Review Board (ARB).[115] The ARB did consider the reduction in the size of the SST and its changed responsibilities, but the board did not interview Lieutenant Colonel Gibson or Rear Admiral Losey.[116] It seems the ARB also did not thoroughly examine the Lieutenant Colonel Gibson's unit's actions on the day of the attack, although the vice chairman, Admiral (ret.) Michael Mullen, may have inquired about its activities later.[117]

VI. The Department of Defense is working to correct many weaknesses revealed by the Benghazi attack, but the global security situation is still deteriorating and military resources continue to decline.

After the Benghazi attack, the Department of Defense organized an internal staff group to evaluate what had transpired and what improvements were needed.[118] The activities of this group in large measure were focused initially on providing information to the ARB.[119] As a second step, the Department engaged the State Department to determine what broader changes were required by what has been termed the "New Normal" security situation in the region.[120] Finally, in May 2013, General Dempsey asked the director of joint force development (J-7) to collect and evaluate the after action review written by each military unit involved.[121]

---

[113] Dustin Walker, "Pentagon: Special Forces Would Not have Saved Lives in Benghazi," *Real Clear Defense*, May 8, 2013.

[114] "Pentagon: Special Forces Would Not have Saved Lives in Benghazi;" and Office of the Secretary of Defense (Legislative Affairs) e-mail to Committee on Armed Services staff, May 8, 2013 (in committee possession). Confusingly, one spokesman specifically "rejected" any suggestion that the four remained behind to provide additional protection for the embassy in Tripoli. See "Pentagon: Special Forces Would Not have Saved Lives in Benghazi."

[115] For the ARB staff size, see Transcript, U.S. House of Representatives, Committee on Oversight and Government Reform, "Interview of: Admiral Michael Mullen," June 19, 2013 (hereafter "Mullen Interview"), p. 18; and reply to Question for the Record submitted to Under Secretary of State Patrick Kennedy by Edward Royce, Chairman, Committee on Foreign Affairs, September 18, 2013 (in committee possession).

[116] AFRICOM and SOCAFRICA Briefing, pp. 91, 130, 134; Mullen Interview, pp. 100-103,

[117] Mullen Interview, pp. 55-56, 91-97, and 147-148 This point is further confused as shown in the Oversight Committee's deposition of Ambassador Thomas Pickering, the ARB chairman. (See Transcript, U.S. House of Representatives, Committee on Oversight and Government Reform, "Deposition of: Ambassador Thomas R. Pickering," June 4, 2013, pp. 99-101.) For General Dempsey's assumption about the ARB's knowledge, see Dempsey Briefing, p. 36. For other details on Admiral Mullen's work and the ARB process, see Mullen Interview, pp. 16, 21-23, 29-31; and Hearing Transcript, U.S. House of Representatives, Committee on Oversight and Government Reform, "Reviews of Benghazi Attack and Unanswered Questions," September 19, 2013.

[118] May Benghazi Briefing, Part II, p. 49

[119] September Lessons Learned Hearing, p. 47.

[120] Dempsey Briefing, pp. 29, 37.

[121] Dempsey Briefing, pp. 29-30, 44.

The committee has received and reviewed this classified assessment and seven underlying documents. The majority members agree that compiling and considering these reports is an important function for the Department to undertake. They offer a good summary of the extent of the Department's knowledge of events and perpetrators and changes instituted since the attacks. They also contain various minor and apparently immaterial inaccuracies and myriad details extraneous to the committee's evaluation.[122]

In assessing the lessons learned, General Dempsey told the committee

we are better postured today, but the risk is higher today. And, so I remain concerned that events of this nature, unless there is a threat stream that allows us to prepare, or if those responsible on the ground in the embassy can take decisions early enough to either let us thicken the ranks or withdraw them, we remain at risk.[123]

As Mr. Reid similarly summarized, "[i]n places where the threat is high and the host nation's capacity is low or our facility is vulnerable, the Department of Defense can be a bridging solution by either providing temporary forces . . . or by enhancing the posture of nearby response forces and assets until those risks are brought to a more manageable level by permanent solutions."[124]

The Department is attempting to improve its ability to respond to a Benghazi-like scenario. "I want to underscore," Mr. Reid declared to the committee, "that we are more ready than ever to respond to a crisis or attack if one occurs without warning."[125] "[T]ailored response forces" are now located closer to "the area of most anticipated need," he said. They are also equipped with the necessary transports. This means that, unlike Benghazi, their dispatch is not contingent upon the arrival of these planes.[126]

Furthermore, the New Normal outlook is intended to yield an improved force laydown set amidst a broader interagency understanding of which diplomatic outposts are considered high risk, and what security improvements or emergency response capabilities are consequently possible to serve those locations. While the preference is for host governments to offer better protection to U.S. facilities, in those instances in which they are incapable of doing so, the Department of Defense can assign additional security forces or reposition its rapid response units. In general, however, Defense leaders believe peremptorily increasing U.S. military presence in a particular location is preferable to being forced to dispatch emergency units once a crisis erupts.[127]

---

[122] The Department noted in the letter conveying the document that it consists of "unit-level reports based on information available to the unit at the time of preparation, and may reflect out-of-date or inaccurate information." See Lieutenant General David L. Goldfein, Director, Joint Staff, letter to Howard P. "Buck" McKeon, Chairman, Committee on Armed Services, December 6, 2013.

[123] Dempsey Briefing, pp. 46-47.

[124] September Lessons Learned Hearing, p. 15.

[125] May Benghazi Briefing, Part I, pp. 44-45; and September Lessons Learned Hearing, pp. 16 (quotation) and 18.

[126] September Lessons Learned Hearing, p. 22.

[127] September Lessons Learned Hearing, pp. 12, 16, 19, and Senate Hearing.

Improvements to Marine Corps capabilities

Although previously there was also great reliance on indigenous forces helping to protect American diplomatic outposts, Mr. Reid told the committee, "[c]learly we have a different mindset today than we had then."[128] While Marines assigned to embassies in past years were charged primarily with guarding classified information and equipment (not necessarily fending off an attack), the Department has since given them these broader responsibilities along with additional specialized weaponry and extra training. There was no Marine Security Guard detachment in Libya in 2012. By the end of 2014, thirty-five U.S. diplomatic facilities similarly without this protection will receive the units. Furthermore, the size of existing detachments in twenty-seven "high-threat, high risk" posts is being increased.[129]

The prepositioning and status of the FAST platoons has also changed since the Benghazi attack. Secretary Panetta said in February 2012, "[w]e've located them in key areas. We've reduced their response time [and w]e now have airlift associated with them."[130] In addition, the Department has established a "crisis response" Marine Air-Ground Task Force (MAGTF) to go to trouble spots.[131] Indeed, General Dempsey told the House Armed Services Committee that since April, various "response forces" have had their alert level increased "approximately 85 times" and elements have moved closer to a danger zone on 26 occasions.[132]

Commander's In-Extremis Force (CIF)

At the time of the Benghazi attack, AFRICOM did not have its own CIF. Instead, it shared a CIF with the European Command, and this unit was tasked to respond to the Benghazi attacks.[133] Nonetheless, the Libyan events seem to have spurred some reassessment of the capabilities, basing, and response posture of CIFs across all Combatant Commands. Although preparations began before the Benghazi attack, an AFRICOM CIF was established formally in October 2012. Nonetheless, General Ham testified before the Senate in March 2013 that this unit still lacked certain intelligence, aviation, other capabilities. He also noted that most assigned personnel were in Colorado. A contingent was deployed in Europe, but according to General Ham, no element had yet been stationed in Africa. Although General Ham noted the ease in which components assigned to southern Europe could respond across northern Africa, events in Benghazi suggest this is problematic.[134]

---

[128] May Benghazi Briefing, Part I, p. 36. For General Ham's endorsement of increasing the capabilities of indigenous forces, see AFRICOM and SOCAFRICA Briefing, p. 62.

[129] May Benghazi Briefing, Part I, pp. 44, 69; September Lessons Learned Hearing, pp. 13-14; and Dempsey Briefing, p. 7.

[130] Senate Hearing.

[131] May Benghazi Briefing, Part I, pp. 44-45; Aspen Remarks.

[132] Dempsey Briefing, p. 7. According to press reports, portions of the MAGTF moved from Moron, Spain to Djibouti in December 2013 in preparation for guarding and/or evacuating Americans from strife-torn South Sudan. Rear Admiral John F. Kirby, the DOD spokesman, specifically cited the "lessons learned from the tragic events in Benghazi" when describing this movement to the press. See Karen Young and Sudarsan Raghavan, "Marines in position to aid in possible S. Sudan evacuation," *Washington Post*, December 23, 2013.

[133] DOD timeline; and Senate Hearing, p. 9.

[134] Hearing Transcript, U.S. Senate, Committee on Armed Services, "U.S. Africa command and U.S. Transportation Command in Review of the Defense Authorization Request for FY 2014 and Future Years Defense Program," March 7, 2013.

Continued limitations to the military's ability to respond in absence of coherent U.S. strategy for the region and declining resources

The National Defense Authorization Act for fiscal year 2014 requires the Secretary of Defense (in consultation with the chairman of the Joint Chiefs of Staff and the Secretary of State) to convey a report to the committee on lessons learned from the Benghazi attack. The report must assess the military's posture and readiness, describe the ability of the U.S. military to respond to requests from the Department of State for supplemental embassy security forces, and identify possible related intelligence enhancements.[135]

Yet, there are disturbing indications that the administration has yet to develop an adequate approach to address the dramatic events that are convulsing the greater Middle East. Majority members believe that in spite of the military's efforts to incorporate lessons learned from the attack, growing violence and instability continue to endanger our diplomats and pose significant threats to U.S. security. Almost daily, news accounts provide overwhelming evidence that Al Qaeda and its affiliates and other terrorist groups still pose grave threats to the United States and its allies in the Mideast. These conditions also lay the groundwork for potentially even more dire future challenges.

General David Rodriguez, AFRICOM's current commander, for example, acknowledged to the *New York Times* recently that U.S. forces "face serious threats in Africa from a range of extremist groups, including two Al Qaeda affiliates," and noted that new terrorist groups are on the rise.[136] In Egypt, increasing tensions between the military and Muslim Brotherhood have resulted in instability and violence, including car bombings and other attacks in Cairo.[137] Finally, a resurgence of al Qaeda in Iraq threatens to spark further violence across the region, with "grave implications on U.S. national security interests," according to one former U.S. official.[138]

Unfortunately, it is within this ominous security environment that the President and Congress continue to under-resource the military. Uncertainty about available resources significantly inhibits military planning and leads to decision-making about force lay down that tends to prioritize cost over operational effectiveness. Indeed, the president's budget request for national security functions has declined every year he has been in office. This trend is expected to continue in Fiscal Year 2015. Should sequestration fail to be resolved, the funding for the military will have been reduced by more than $1.3 trillion through Fiscal Year 2021. Indeed, it has already been cut by over $800 billion in the last four years.

Moreover, keeping State Department personnel safe is but one element of an effort of a broader defense plan. It is essential that the U.S. adopt again a sound and sustainable defense strategy that funds DOD at levels that allows the U.S. military to confront the world's dangers. The majority members acknowledge the significant capabilities available to the U.S. military, as

---

[135] "National Defense Authorization Act for Fiscal Year 2014," Pub. L. No. 113-66, §12431.

[136] Eric Schmitt, "U.S. Mission in South Sudan Shows Limits of Military," *New York Times*, January 9, 2014.

[137] Abigail Hauslohner, "In Egypt, Many Shrug as Freedoms Disappear," *Washington Post*, January 8, 2014.

[138] David Ignatius, "Iran's Fingerprints in Fallujah," *Washington Post*, January 8, 2014.

well as the extraordinary dedication and commitment of our service members. Yet, the Department of Defense cannot be expected to prevent or respond to the full range of growing threats, especially as funding declines. In considering the President's forthcoming spending plan and in evaluating how currently authorized money is being allocated, the committee intends, on a bipartisan basis, to continue to assess if the nation's defense strategy is sound and to advocate for additional resources for critical national security functions.

Note on the Participation of Defense Department Briefers and Interviewees

DOD is making civilian officials and current or retired military members readily available to the committee. Briefers and interviewees are appearing willingly at the committee's request, but have not been sworn in, in keeping with the committee's standard practice.[139] Furthermore, in response to a specific query about "non-disclosure agreements," a senior Defense official has made clear in correspondence with committee that the "Department has not requested nor required relevant personnel to sign any such agreement since the attacks."[140] Information provided by those appearing before the committee have been consistent with this assertion.[141]

Lieutenant Colonel Gibson told the committee he was instructed if he received "any questions" from any source about Benghazi, he was "to direct [his interlocutors] to AFRICOM." He noted Defense Department staffers "did review" an opening statement he delivered to the committee, but they did not exercise "editorial rights over it."[142] Regardless, his subsequent colloquy with the committee continued without interruption and was not limited to the contents of his prepared statement.

---

[139] In addition to the general legal requirement to provide truthful information to Congress, military members have taken an oath to "support and defend the Constitution of the United States." (See 18 U.S. Code §1001.) Many risk their lives doing so. In light of this commitment and prevailing legal strictures, the committee deems a separate oath to be unnecessary.

[140] Elizabeth King, Assistant Secretary of Defense (Legislative Affairs) letter to Howard P. "Buck" McKeon, Chairman, Committee on Armed Services, July 30, 2013. Colonel George Bristol also declared, "I have neither been asked to, nor signed any nondisclosure agreements." (See July Benghazi Briefing, p. 9.)

[141] When General Dempsey was asked directly when appearing before the committee, "[d]id you order or tell or suggest" that anyone "not talk to Congress?" he answered, "[n]o." He added, "I've never been made aware of any order to, in any way, discourage anyone from being anything other than completely forthright with this committee and others." (See Dempsey Briefing, pp. 14-15.) "Absolutely not," is how Rear Admiral Losey replied when similarly queried. (See AFRICOM and SOCAFRICA Briefing, p. 114.)

[142] AFRICOM and SOCAFRICA Briefing, p. 93.